What Do You Find in a Backyard?

Megan Kopp

Crabtree Publishing Company

www.crabtreebooks.com

Ecosystems Close-Up

Author
Megan Kopp

Publishing plan research and development
Reagan Miller

Editors
Janine Deschenes
Crystal Sikkens

Design
Ken Wright
Tammy McGarr (cover)

Photo research
Janine Deschenes
Crystal Sikkens

Production coordinator and prepress technician
Ken Wright

Print coordinator
Katherine Berti

Illustrations
Bonna Rouse: pages 5, 21

Photographs
iStockphoto: page 8
All other images from Shutterstock

Library and Archives Canada Cataloguing in Publication

Kopp, Megan, author
    What do you find in a backyard? / Megan Kopp.

(Ecosystems close-up)
Includes index.
Issued in print and electronic formats.
ISBN 978-0-7787-2255-7 (bound).--ISBN 978-0-7787-2267-0 (paperback).--
ISBN 978-1-4271-1722-9 (html)

1. Suburban animals--Juvenile literature. 2. Urban animals--Juvenile
literature. 3. Urban ecology (Biology)--Juvenile literature. I. Title.

QH541.5.C6K67 2016   j591.75'6   C2015-907986-1
                                               C2015-907987-X

Library of Congress Cataloging-in-Publication Data

Names: Kopp, Megan, author.
Title: What do you find in a backyard? / Megan Kopp.
Description: New York, New York : Crabtree
  Publishing Company, [2016] | Series: Ecosystems close-up | Includes
  index.
  | Description based on print version record and CIP data provided by
  publisher; resource not viewed.
Identifiers: LCCN 2015045730 (print) | LCCN 2015045152 (ebook) | ISBN
  9781427117229 (electronic HTML) | ISBN 9780778722557 (reinforced
  library binding : alk. paper) | ISBN 9780778722670 (pbk. : alk. paper)
Subjects: LCSH: Urban ecology (Biology)--Juvenile literature. | Urban
  animals--Juvenile literature. | Garden ecology--Juvenile literature. |
  Garden animals--Juvenile literature.
Classification: LCC QH541.5.C6 (print) | LCC QH541.5.C6 K67 2016
  (ebook) | DDC 578.75/6--dc23
LC record available at http://lccn.loc.gov/2015045730

Crabtree Publishing Company

Printed in Canada/032016/EF20160210

www.crabtreebooks.com   1-800-387-7650

Published in Canada
Crabtree Publishing
616 Welland Ave.
St. Catharines, Ontario
L2M 5V6

Published in the United States
Crabtree Publishing
PMB 59051
350 Fifth Avenue, 59th Floor
New York, New York 10118

Published in the United Kingdom
Crabtree Publishing
Maritime House
Basin Road North, Hove
BN41 1WR

Published in Australia
Crabtree Publishing
3 Charles Street
Coburg North
VIC 3058

Contents

What is a Backyard?

Backyards are made up of both living and nonliving things. In backyards, the Sun shines, air moves, soil covers the ground, and rain falls from the sky. These are nonliving things in a backyard.

The types of living things found in a backyard depend on the weather.

apple tree

fence

birdhouse

grass

birdfeeder

birds

*Scientists use **models**, such as this drawing of a northern U.S. backyard, to help us understand how things are connected.*

water

birdbath

flowers

What's in your Backyard?

In North America, backyards are often full of life. Plants and animals are living things. You might find grass, flowers, or trees in a North American backyard. Insects buzz around. Birds chirp. Squirrels chatter.

A Backyard Ecosystem

A system is made up of connected parts that work together. An **ecosystem** is a system made up of all the living and nonliving things found in one place. A backyard is a type of ecosystem.

Robins need earthworms and insects for food. They can meet this need in a backyard ecosystem.

Backyard Living

Plants and animals are living things. Living things grow. As they grow, living things change and create new living things. Animals have babies. Plants create new plants. All plants need sunlight, air, and water to grow. Animals need water, air, food, and **shelter** to survive.

Let the Sun Shine in!

Backyards are normally open spaces with a lot of sunlight. Sunlight is important for trees and other backyard plants. Every plant needs sunlight, air, and water to make their own food. Food gives them **energy** to grow.

The Sun helps trees make their own food so they can grow tall.

Growing green grass

Grass is one of the most common plants in North American backyards. When sunlight reaches the grass, it can grow to cover your whole backyard.

Take a Deep Breath

All living things need air to survive. Air is a nonliving thing. It is found all around a backyard. The animals that live there get air in different ways.

Did you know there is air in dirt? Earthworms breathe it through their skin.

What do you Think?

How well do you think these animals would survive if they could not take in enough air?

Gills allow fish to take in air from the water.

A Need for Air

Birds and squirrels breathe through lungs. Insects breathe through a row of holes along their bodies. Have you ever seen a fishpond in a backyard? Fish breathe through special body parts called **gills**.

A Thirsty Backyard

All living things need water. Most backyard plants get water from rain. Some of the rain that falls from clouds soaks into the soil on the ground. Trees and other plants have roots that suck up the water from the soil.

roots

What do you Think?

Do you think many plants could survive in a dry, desert backyard? Why or why not?

12

Drink up!

Animals meet their need for water in many different ways. Earthworms soak up water through their skin. Squirrels get some of the water they need from their food. Robins also get water from the food they eat, such as juicy berries. Other animals drink water from puddles, pools, or birdbaths.

Bats drink water from backyard ponds and creeks at night.

Feed me!

All living things in a backyard ecosystem need food. Food gives living things the energy they need to live and grow. Plants make their own food using sunlight, air, and water.

Some backyard birds, such as these white-crowned sparrows, get their food from bird feeders.

Munching on lunch

Animals can't make their own food. They get their energy from other living things. Some animals eat plants. Grasshoppers munch on backyard flowers for energy. Some animals eat other animals. Bluebirds eat grasshoppers. A **food chain** shows the flow of energy from one living thing to another in an ecosystem.

What do you Think?

How do bluebirds depend on backyard flowers to live?

This picture is an example of a backyard food chain. The arrows show the flow of energy.

Home, Tweet Home

All animals need shelter to survive. Rocks, leaves, trees, and fallen logs are all types of shelters. Sometimes, these places are used to hide from other animals. Other times, animals use shelters to lay eggs or have babies.

Squirrels use holes in trees for shelter.

Some birds use human-made structures such as nest boxes for shelter.

What do you Think?

Are animal shelters living things, nonliving things, or both?

Staying Safe

Ants dig tunnels underground to avoid birds that want to eat them. Squirrels build nests high in trees for protection. Birds lay eggs in nests built in many backyard trees.

A Helping Hand

Backyards can be fun places to play. They can be good places to grow flowers and vegetables. They can also be good places for wild things to live and grow. Backyards with different kinds of trees and flowers meet the needs of many animals.

Nest boxes, bird feeders, and birdbaths are helpful for wildlife.

Research how to build a shelter in your backyard to attract insects and small animals.

Watch for Wildlife

Plant a bush that makes berries and you might see flocks of berry-eating birds. Sunflowers and bird feeders bring in birds that eat seeds. Create a garden with a lot of flowers and you will see different kinds of butterflies.

Create a Space

A model is a **representation** of a real thing. Models can explain how different parts of a system work together. Pictures, storyboards, maps, and diagrams are all kinds of models.

You can make a model to show what living things need to survive in a backyard ecosystem.

Make a Model

To make your model, draw a diagram of your backyard or the backyard of someone you know.

tree

apples

birdfeeder

birdfeeder

birdhouse

grass

birdfeeder

squirrel

birds

birdseed

water

birdbath

flowers

Label the living and nonliving things on your model. You can also label different shelters and possible food sources.

Sharing the System

Present your model to your classmates. Show what parts of the diagram are nonliving things. Explain how the living things in your diagram need nonliving things to survive. Show how living things also need other living things.

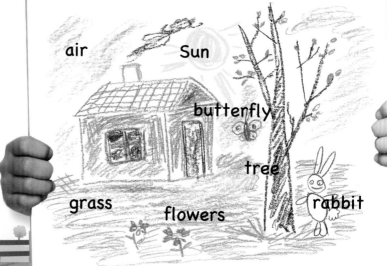

Help your classmates understand how your backyard ecosystem meets the needs of the different plants and animals.

air

Sun

butterfly

tree

grass

flowers

rabbit

Learning more

Books

LeBlanc Cate, Annette. *Look Up!: Bird-Watching in Your Own Backyard*. Candlewick Press, 2013.

Root, Phyllis. *Plant a Pocket of Prairie.* University Press, 2014.

Weidner Zoehfeld, Kathleen. *Secrets of the Garden: Food Chains and the Food Web in Our Backyard.* Knopf Books for Young Readers, 2012.

Websites

Backyard Nature
www.backyardnature.net

National Wildlife Federation: Garden for Wildlife
www.nwf.org/how-to-help/garden-for-wildlife/create-a-habitat.aspx

National Wildife Federation: Backyard Scavenger Hunt
www.nwf.org/kids/family-fun/outdoor-activities/ backyard-scavenger-hunt.aspx

Santa Barbara Museum of Natural History:
A Kid's Guide to Backyard Critters
www.sbnature.org/content/663/file/backyardcrittersMar2011.pdf

Words to know

ecosystem (EE-koh-sis-tuhm) noun All the living and nonliving things in a place and their relation to the environment

energy (EN-er-jee) noun Something living things need to live, move, and grow

food chain (food cheyn) noun The order of living things in an ecosystem by which food energy is passed from one to another

gill (gil) noun A special body part which allows fish and other animals to breathe underwater

model (MOD-l) noun A representation of a real object

representation (rep-ri-zen-TEY-shuhn) noun A picture, drawing, model, or other copy of something

shelter (SHEL-ter) noun The place where living things are protected

survive (ser-VAHYV) verb To stay alive

A *noun* is a person, place, or thing. A *verb* is an action word that tells you what someone or something does.

Index